L I F E ' S   G O L D E N   R U L E S™

Polite Society

The Golden Rules for Modern Etiquette

compiled by
Raechel Donahue

GENERAL PUBLISHING GROUP
Los Angeles

The Life's Golden Rules™ series is published by General Publishing Group, Inc., 2701 Ocean Park Boulevard, Suite 140, CA 90405, 310-314-4000

Library of Congress Catalog Number 95-75019
ISBN 1-881649-13-X

10 9 8 7 6 5 4 3 2 1

Colby Allerton, Editor
Cover Design by Catherine Vo Bailey

PRINTED IN THE USA

Polite Society

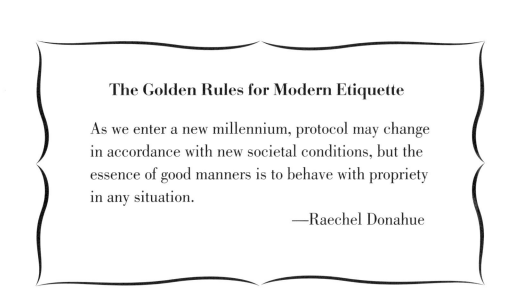

The Golden Rules for Modern Etiquette

As we enter a new millennium, protocol may change in accordance with new societal conditions, but the essence of good manners is to behave with propriety in any situation.

—Raechel Donahue

1 ❖ The best response to a compliment, no matter how exaggerated, is a simple "thank you."

2 ❖ Never serve a guest a beverage in a chipped glass. The lawsuit could be ruinous.

3 ❖ It is perfectly appropriate for a woman to hold a door open for a man, and vice versa.

4 ✦ Don't worry so much about the order of introductions, just try to get everyone's name right.

5 ✦ Remembering someone's name is the height of all good manners.

6 ✦ Always use your mate's name during introductions. All too often people merely say, "And this is my wife/husband."

7 ✦ A raised voice to people in the service industry is not only in poor taste, but it rarely accomplishes anything.

8 ✦ Thank you notes should be handwritten and promptly sent.

9 ✦ In addressing correspondence to a married woman, include her first name: "Mrs. Jane Somebody," rather than "Mrs. John Somebody."

10 ✦ Always determine the field of someone's Ph.D. before introducing them to your friends as "Doctor."

11 ✦ When in a group, everyone should be included in the conversation.

12 ✦ Regardless of how proud a mother may be, she should know which places (like movie theaters and adult parties) are inappropriate for infants.

13 ✦ A faxed letter should always be followed with a mailed original.

14 ✦ Do not dismiss people who drive beat up economy cars. They could be doing it for the sake of the environment.

15 ✦ Ferraris are only socially acceptable if one owns enough open road in the country on which to run them.

16 ✦ After you ask a question, listen to the answer.

17 ✦ Fight the temptation to interrupt or finish other people's sentences for them.

18 ✦ Old clothing should be washed, folded and donated to a charity or thrift shop—not thrown away.

19 ✦ Cloth napkins not only make the most proper table setting, but are environmentally and economically sound.

20 ✦ "Please" should always precede a request, even when speaking with children.

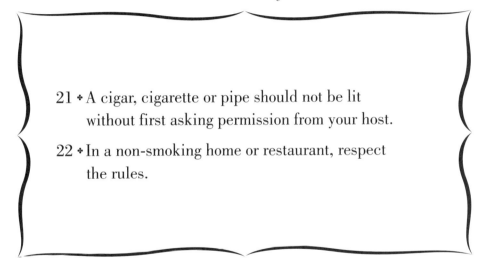

21 ✦ A cigar, cigarette or pipe should not be lit without first asking permission from your host.

22 ✦ In a non-smoking home or restaurant, respect the rules.

23 ✦ A message left on an answering machine should be as brief as possible as a courtesy to those who must retrieve their messages by remote.

24 ✦ Personal messages left on E–mail may prove to be embarrassing for both parties.

25 ✦ Tasting champagne in a restaurant is not necessary. If it has turned, it'll be flat.

26 ✦ "Tea" includes scones, cucumber sandwiches, meringue cookies and the like.

27 ✦ "High tea" is more like a simple supper, including cold meats or perhaps eggs.

28 ✦ If you return to the table from the salad bar before your dinner companions, wait for their return before beginning to eat.

29 ✦ If you are on a special diet and are hosting a dinner in a restaurant, be sure to urge your guests to order freely.

30 ✦ When arranging a buffet table, do not put the desserts on the same table with the entrees.

31 ✦ In the matter of gift giving, pay close attention to the tastes of the recipient. A year's supply of steaks sent to a vegetarian is unacceptable.

32 ✦ Guests at a dinner party have no business inquiring what's going to be served. If you don't like it, don't eat it.

33 ✦ Business entertainment is an oxymoron.

34 ✤ A man concerned about making an improper remark to a woman should think how he would feel if a woman said the same thing to him.

35 ✦ Unless the person entering the room is actually in the show you're watching, turn off the television when someone arrives.

36 ✦ Compliments are always appreciated.

37 ✦ If answering a dating ad, arrange for cocktails or coffee. Whoever placed the ad, pays.

38 ✦ Be sure to have non-alcoholic drinks available at a cocktail party.

39 ✦ Call waiting should be used sparingly, if at all.

40 ✦ If you use your car phone to help someone in an emergency, don't ask them to pay for the call.

41 ✦ Carry no more than two pieces of luggage on an airplane, and one should be a briefcase.

42 ✦ If you can smell your own cologne ten minutes after application, you are wearing too much.

43 ✦ Unless you know them, never approach celebrities who are dining privately.

44 ✦ Courtesy never goes out of style.

45 ✦ When entertaining, be yourself and enjoy others
being themselves.

46 ✦ It is appropriate to discuss someone's salary only
when you are his or her employer.

47 ✤ Always be prepared to tip restroom attendants, as that is often how they make their living.

48 ✤ Tip twenty percent to the driver of a rented limousine.

49 ✤ If someone sends a car for you, it is not necessary to tip the driver.

50 ✦ Any extra service request of hotel personnel, such as extra towels, requires a gratuity.

51 ✦ A house sitter should leave the place immaculate, and should also leave wine or flowers.

52 ✦ Always bring a small gift for your host if spending the night or the weekend.

53 ✦ "Two things stink after three days—
fish and house guests."

—Ben Franklin

54 ✦ If the drinks are on the house or the host, tip generously.

55 ✦ If you are displeased with the food at a restaurant, don't take it out on the waiter, speak to the manager.

56 ✦ If you're paying for an expensive meal and it is unsatisfactory, by all means complain.

57 ✦ It is pointless to complain about a cheap meal.

58 ✦ A tip to a headwaiter or hostess can move your name closer to the top of the list in a restaurant that doesn't take reservations.

59 ✦ When tipping a headwaiter, fold the bill so the denomination shows.

60 ✦ If you see a crime in progress, report it. It is no longer acceptable to "not get involved."

61 ✦ It's okay to scream if your purse has been snatched.

62 ✦ Always give money to street musicians unless they are completely without talent.

63 ✦ McDonald's certificates are appropriate donations to the soliciting homeless.

64 ✦ Class is something you're born into; style is something you acquire.

65 ✦ Great wealth does not excuse poor manners.

66 ✦ A gentleman is someone who knows how to play the accordion, but doesn't.

67 ✦ Conspicuous consumption is no longer a sign of good breeding.

68 ✦ "Class is something that dissolves very quickly in alcohol."   —Raymond Chandler

69 ✦ Always include your telephone number on answering machine messages.

70 ✦ Neither undertip nor overtip.

71 ✦ Do unto others as you would have others do unto you.

72 ✦ Resist the impulse to give the one finger salute to rude drivers.

73 ✦ Talking in the movies is not only rude, it's a waste of money and time.

74 ✦ In foreign countries, speaking louder in the wrong language does nothing to improve communication.

75 ✦ Domestic quarrels should not take place in public.

76 ✦ "If you want an audience, start a fight."

—Gaelic proverb

77 ✦ Treat police officers respectfully and they will respond in kind.

78 ✦ Arrogance is always rude.

79 ✦ Be polite to the rude. It drives them crazy.

80 ✦ Never bring an extra guest to a party without first checking with your host.

81 ✦ Be sure to have the right change before boarding public transportation, including taxis.

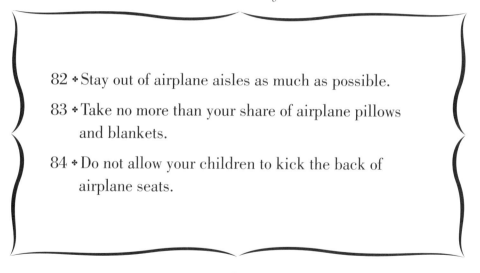

82 ✦ Stay out of airplane aisles as much as possible.

83 ✦ Take no more than your share of airplane pillows and blankets.

84 ✦ Do not allow your children to kick the back of airplane seats.

85 ✦ Don't sing while wearing airplane headphones.

86 ✦ Respect the privacy of airplane seat mates and
they'll respect yours.

87 ✦ In public places it is generally best to resist
acting on primal urges.

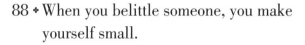

88 ✤ When you belittle someone, you make yourself small.

89 ✤ Never presume to know another's sexual preference unless told first hand.

90 ✦ If you keep your nose in the air, you may drown in the rain.

91 ✦ Your wallet only makes you a bigger person if you're standing on it.

92 ✦ Be honest without being brutally frank.

93 ✦ "It is far more impressive when
others discover your good qualities
without your help."

—Miss Manners (Judith Martin)

94 ✦ At a party, avoid monopolizing the conversation.

95 ✦ "A lady is one who never shows her underwear
   unintentionally."   —Lillian Day

96 ✦ Never mistake endurance for hospitality.

97 ✦ Even if you have an opinion on everything, it's
   not always necessary to give it.

98 ✦ "Good breeding consists of concealing how much we think of ourselves and how little we think of the other person."   —Mark Twain

99 ✤ If you make a confidential aside in a foreign language, never assume that no one else in earshot can understand it.

100 ✤ All actions have consequences.

101 ✤ Learn the Ten Golden Rules.

102 ✤ Conversations opened with "I'll bet you don't remember me" usually don't go far.

103 ✤ Unannounced visitors are most often unwelcome.

104 ✤ A dinner party is one of those events to which it is unforgivable to be fashionably late.

105 ✤ If the conversation is lagging, bring up the subject of food.

106 ✦ "Actually, that's rather a private matter," is preferable to "None of your beeswax."

107 ✦ Those who talk the way they think should think more often.

108 ✦ Never be the last one to leave.

109 ✦ Your perfume should not announce your imminent arrival nor should it remain after your departure.

110 ✦ "If people turn to look at you on the street, you are not well dressed." —Beau Brummel

111 ✦ Men should remove their gloves before shaking hands, although it is not considered necessary for women.

112 ✦ Pearls are always appropriate, except perhaps with a bathing suit.

113 ✦ Gifts of wine or food are intended to be consumed
after you have left the home of your host or hostess.

114 ✦ Home grown tomatoes are always a welcome gift.

115 ✦ At a dinner party, vegetarians should not complain, but enjoy extra helpings of bread or vegetables.

116 ✦ It's not so important that you know which fork to use, but that you know when to use a fork.

117 ✦ The napkin goes on the left.

118 ✦ The bread plate should be to the left of the dinner plate.

119 ✦ Chopsticks should be placed horizontally across the top of the bowl or on a chopsticks rest.

120 ✦ Don't call a woman "honey" unless you know her personally.

121 ✦ A man walks behind a woman going up a staircase, but precedes her when descending.

122 ✦ Loyalty is the glue that holds relationships together.

123 ✦ "Leave a hotel room as you would leave a room if you had a valued maid who would quit if pushed too far." —Miss Manners (Judith Martin)

124 ✦ Do not tip airline attendants, bus drivers or elevator operators.

125 ✦ Tip a delivery person at least a buck a pizza.

126 ✦ Don't tip ship's officers.

127 ✦ If you've borrowed a yacht, tip the captain.

128 ❖ Cellular phones should not be taken inside
restaurants or theaters, and your beeper should
be placed on "vibrate" if you can't turn it off.

129 ✦ Do not bring uninvited guests. Anywhere.

130 ✦ Good manners have nothing to do with money.

131 ✦ Even if it looks like a mansion, it should
always be called a home.

132 ✦ Never park in handicapped parking spaces.

133 ✦ Even children should know that physically or
    mentally challenged people deserve courtesy
    and respect.

134 ✦ If they need assistance, most handicapped people
    will ask for it. Leave the option open.

135 ❖ Show no more than one baby picture unless upon request.

136 ❖ Good manners come more easily when learned at an early age.

137 ✦ Religious and political beliefs should not be
forced on others in a social situation.

138 ✦ Never disparage another's religious beliefs.

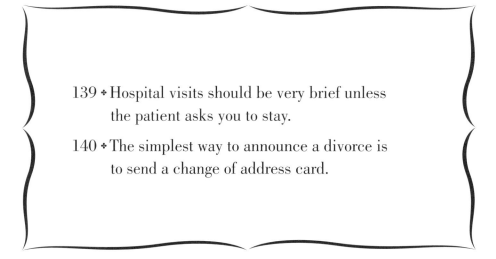

139 ✦ Hospital visits should be very brief unless the patient asks you to stay.

140 ✦ The simplest way to announce a divorce is to send a change of address card.

141 ✤ The only way to eat ribs is with your fingers and a lot of napkins.

142 ✤ Never try to chew the oyster in an oyster shooter.

143 ✤ "Never eat more than you can lift."

—Miss Piggy

144 ✤ Do not approach a celebrity by saying, "Aren't you somebody?"

145 ✤ Telling tales about your personal life on a television talk show is nearly always a breach of etiquette.

146 ✤ Only situations of crushing boredom warrant a self-inflicted beeper page.

147 ✤ Never be rude to a tow truck driver if you plan on getting out of your predicament quickly.

148 ✦ People living together should agree on how they will introduce one another socially.

149 ✦ Roommates should never eat food they have not purchased.

150 ✦ In all relationships, the sharing of a bathroom requires superior civility and cooperation.

151 ❖ "Tradition is what you resort to when you
don't have the time or money to do it right."

—Kurt Herbert Adler (1905-1988)

152 ❖ When in doubt, say it tastes just like chicken.

153 ❖ Learn to handle failure and success with
equal grace.

154 ✤ Know how to dress, and when.

155 ✤ "Being perfectly well-dressed gives a feeling of
tranquillity that religion is powerless to bestow."
—Ralph Waldo Emerson

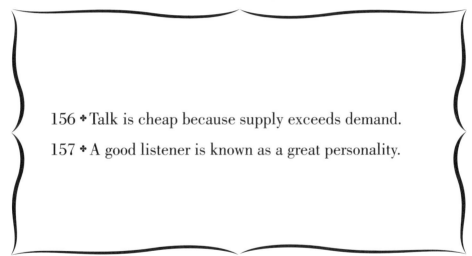

156 ✦ Talk is cheap because supply exceeds demand.

157 ✦ A good listener is known as a great personality.

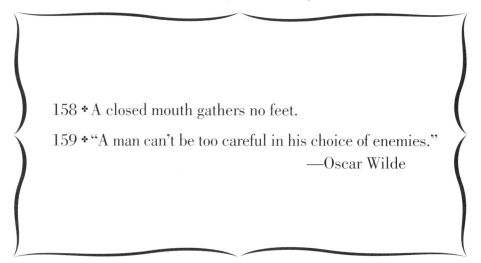

158 ❖ A closed mouth gathers no feet.

159 ❖ "A man can't be too careful in his choice of enemies."

—Oscar Wilde

160 ❖ Anyone who claims to have class, doesn't.

161 ❖ Keep others' secrets. But avoid being secretive yourself—it breeds mistrust.

162 ❖ Friends don't sue friends.

163 ❖ The time to raise one's voice is in the face of unbending injustice.

164 ✤ Most people become much more interesting
when they stop talking about themselves.

165 ✤ The truth is the safest response in a social
situation.

166 ✤ "Some people stay longer in an hour than others
do in a month."

—William Dean Howls (1837-1920)

167 ✤ Once you are old enough to realize you don't know everything, be tolerant of young people who are sure that they do.

168 ✤ Some people are forgiven for always being late. The late George Washington, for instance.

169 ✤ Boasting doesn't make it so; it merely makes for future embarrassment.

170 ❖ Nasal cavities should be explored in private.

171 ❖ Women who need mascara should apply it before attempting to drive an automobile.

172 ❖ "For a single woman, preparing for company means wiping the lipstick off the milk carton."

—Elayne Boosler

173 ❖ Develop a tiny, stifled yawn for guests who will not leave.

174 ✤ Do not admonish anyone, save your own children, for their lack of manners.

175 ✤ If you have knowingly invited a Party Monster, either have sufficient taxi fare or an isolated guest room.

176 ✛ Never try to out-dress the bride at her wedding.

177 ✛ Unless it is the bride's color scheme, black is inappropriate at a wedding, even if you are mourning the loss of the groom.

178 ✛ All brides are beautiful, as are all babies.

179 ✤ It's simpler to find a private place to breast feed a baby than to create a public controversy.

180 ✤ Children should be told the truth in the kindest, most expedient way before they hear it from strangers.

181 ✤ Avoid the temptation to give parents unsolicited advice about their children.

182 ❖ Regardless of their appearance dictated by current fashion, all teenagers should not be considered hooligans.

183 ❖ Never try to eat an artichoke with a fork. This also applies to hot dogs.

184 ❖ Ask permission before bringing a pet to someone's home.

185 ❖ If a guest asks to use your phone, it's fine to inquire, "Do you need to call long distance?"

186 ❖ If a guest stays on your telephone for an unseemly period of time, smilingly deliver a note saying you are expecting an important call.

187 ❖ The telephone, indelicately used, could be perceived as a blunt instrument.

188 ✦ Almost everyone is offended by a form letter from a friend, even with a personalized salutation.

189 ✦ Formal business letters should close with "Very truly yours," or "Yours very truly."

190 ✦ Use "Sincerely yours" instead of "Love and kisses" when the letter might be read by someone else before the intended recipient.

191 ❖ Sometimes the correct answer is, "I have no idea."

192 ❖ Take care in flirting with a married person. It is they who will most likely suffer the consequences.

193 ✦ Too much flattery goes flat.

194 ✦ "I don't know the key to success, but the key to failure is to try to please everybody."

—Bill Cosby

195 ✦ It's always best to be yourself.

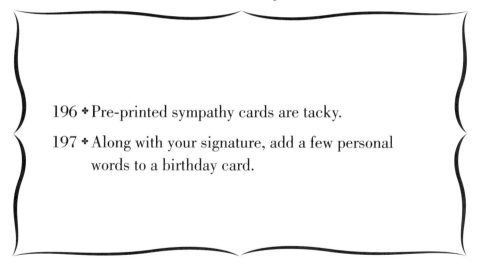

196 ✤ Pre-printed sympathy cards are tacky.

197 ✤ Along with your signature, add a few personal words to a birthday card.

198 ✤ Use "Yes, Sir/Ma'am" to your boss until requested to do otherwise.

199 ✤ A woman in the workplace who doesn't feel that making coffee fits her job description might say, "I've never learned how to do that."

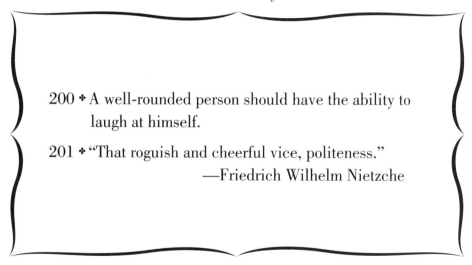

200 ❖ A well-rounded person should have the ability to laugh at himself.

201 ❖ "That roguish and cheerful vice, politeness."
—Friedrich Wilhelm Nietzche

202 ✦ It reflects well upon one who respects his elders and his youngers.

203 ✦ Beware giving a backhanded compliment: "Don't YOU look nice today!" or "For a chubby guy, you don't sweat much."

204 ✤ Vulgar language is de rigueur in some circles. The easily offended should master a couple of obscure foreign phrases that assess the situation.

205 ✤ If you learn no other Latin phrase: "in vino veritas" (in WEE-noh Way-rih-tahs) means "wine loosens the tongue."

206 ✦ Modesty is great power wielded with a soft touch.

207 ✦ Those who are able to do volunteer work should adhere to the same standards as those who are paid for their services.

208 ✦ By definition, charity work does not require pay.

209 ✦ It is improper to call someone at home because you have access to the number through business.

210 ✦ Women especially should ask to see the badge of anyone who claims to be an officer of the law.

211 ✦ The most gracious thing an employer can do is to treat all his employees as equal adults.

212 ❖ No one ever got through to the president of
the company by being rude to the receptionist.

213 ❖ A receptionist should never answer a line with
"Please hold."

214 ❖ If you don't have a good telephone manner,
hire an assistant who does.

215 ✦ "Dear Madam or Sir" may sound old fashioned, but in a letter to a group of unspecified gender, it's better than "You guys."

216 ✦ One should fire an employee in such a way that he or she should be all the way down the elevator before realizing you have not done them a great favor.

217 ✦ The easiest way to avoid charges of sexual harassment in the workplace is to avoid intentional contact with any body part other than the hands.

218 ✤ When leaving in good stead, offer a letter of
resignation which mentions the rewards and
pleasures of your job, for both you and
your employer.

219 ✤ Resigning under protest, write a letter that is
both gracious and telling, though not whining
or accusing.

220 ❖ To lightly flirt with someone else's date is acceptable, but an overt pass is not.

221 ❖ Sarcasm should be reserved for one's closest friends.

222 ❖ Sarcasm should never be used on children. They'll just think you're being snotty.

223 ❖ People who don't have time for visitors should not schedule visitors.

224 ❖ "Let me see if he's in" is not a polite statement.

225 ✦ Genuine emergencies should never be ignored.

226 ✦ Never use "911" on someone's pager unless you have a real emergency or a pre-arranged signal.

227 ❖ A doctor asked for a medical diagnosis at a party may cheerfully say, "Certainly! Would you mind changing into a hospital gown in another room?"

228 ❖ The proper way to rebuff a door-to-door solicitor is, "Thank you, but no."

229 ✤ These days, not all taxi drivers know how to get to where you want to go. Inquire first so as to avoid a later dispute.

230 ✤ Excuses are to be given before an event, not after.

231 ❖ "It is unbecoming for young men to utter maxims."
—Aristotle (384-322 BC)

232 ❖ A direct letter of complaint to a person's superior
is preferable to a thousand hysterical phone calls.

233 ❖ Always try to respect another's feelings.

234 ✦ Mark your luggage with your name, but only your business address, in case your bags are stolen.

235 ✦ Salespeople who appear at your door after 8:30 p.m. should be told to return another time unless you are in desperate need for human contact.

236.✤ Wipe your sweat off the machines in the gym.

237 ✤ In a gym, never make a pass at someone who is in the middle of a set on a machine or free weights.

238 ✤ The only proper way to make a pass at someone who is pressing free weights is to ask if you might act as "spotter."

239 ❖ A gentleman also applies the basic rules of etiquette in single bars.

240 ❖ A woman dining alone isn't necessarily looking for companionship. Send a note with a waiter rather than approaching the table.

241 ✤ A good skier should never ridicule a novice.

242 ✤ The greatest asset of a skier is style.

243 ✤ A talented skier is responsible for avoiding a collision with a beginner—ski slowly through the bunny slopes.

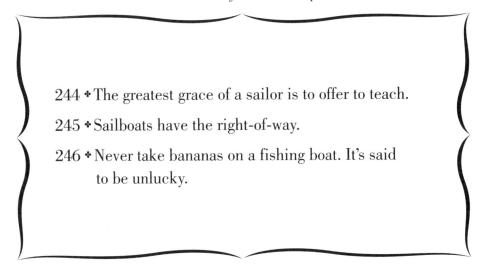

244 ✦ The greatest grace of a sailor is to offer to teach.

245 ✦ Sailboats have the right-of-way.

246 ✦ Never take bananas on a fishing boat. It's said
to be unlucky.

247 ✤ The tasting of wine in a restaurant should not be a sideshow.

248 ❖ The dogless may ask to have their remainders wrapped "to be enjoyed later."

249 ❖ A cockroach sighting in a restaurant should be discreetly mentioned to the management.

250 ❖ Should you see a cockroach or a mouse during dinner at the home of a friend, do your best not to scream. Tell the host much, much later.

251 ✦ The owner of a salon need not be tipped even if he or she has done your hair or nails.

252 ✦ If you wish to separate your social and business affairs, have a calling card for each.

253 ✦ Just because a person does business from the home doesn't mean you may call after normal business hours.

254 ✤ Only friends with a long standing tradition of embarrassing one another may send singing/stripper telegrams to the office.

255 ✤ Never ask a guest to perform at a party without prior arrangement.

256 ✤ Gifts of money should go only to family members and, even then, only when truly appropriate or terribly generous.

257 ✦ In business, respect employees as well as employers.

258 ✦ An office Christmas party should never require the employee to attend alone.

259 ✤ "A little inaccuracy sometimes saves tons of explanation."   —Saki (1870-1916)

260 ✤ One can never err by sending a note of acknowledgment or thanks.

261 ✤ Gossip is second hand smoke.

262 ✤ One of the few forms of acceptable fashion advice to a woman: "Your tag/slip is showing."

263 ✤ Unless you saw him put it on when he was getting dressed, do not offer to straighten a man's tie.

264 ✤ The person with the expense account is the one who should pay for the business lunch.

265 ✦ Do not accept an invitation for another person, even your spouse.

266 ✦ Respect the request for an R.S.V.P.

267 ✦ If you don't R.S.V.P., don't show up.

268 ✦ An invitation is not a summons, merely a request that may be denied.

269 ✤ Be judicious in whom you ask to buy a ridiculous dress in order to be in your wedding.

270 ✤ There is no getting around it: a bride has to send a thank you note to everyone.

271 ✤ There is a reason for a wedding rehearsal. It is the last chance to call it off in relative privacy.

272 ✢ A woman who breaks the engagement must return the ring.

273 ✢ When a man breaks the engagement, the woman is still obligated to return the ring, although not before she makes him sweat a bit.

274 ✤ Social position is not an excuse for ignorance.

275 ✤ The proper compliment for a friend who has appeared in a truly rotten movie is, "You were the best thing in it."

276 ✣ Ultimately, it is more important to do good than to look good.

277 ✣ Friends may come and go, but enemies tend to accumulate. So be nice.

278 ✤ "Never argue with people who buy ink by
    the gallon."   —Tommy Lasorda

279 ✤ The most important social asset is a conscience.

280 ✤ Do not say "Let's have lunch" unless you mean it.

281 ✢ A pregnant bride deserves double blessing.

282 ✢ Having agreed to attend a wedding, one must attend and participate with enthusiasm.

283 ✤ The only relationship that is properly terminated by a letter is one between pen pals.

284 ✤ Do not hang up on a computer-generated sales pitch. Place the receiver on the table and do something else for ten minutes. During that time, the machine can't annoy anyone else.

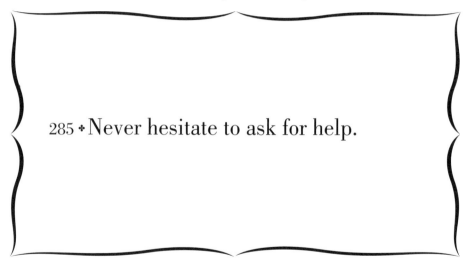

285 ✤ Never hesitate to ask for help.

286 ❖ Each of us is responsible for doing at least one
thing to help preserve our environment.

287 ❖ A minimum of 10% of one's income should be
spent on charity.

288 ✤ Even if we will never want for anything, it does not behoove us to waste our natural resources.

289 ✤ Selfish behavior slowly erodes self-respect.

290 ✤ When asked to a formal event, wear formal attire.

291 ✤ Women need not necessarily wear what is
    currently in fashion.

292 ✤ Only in sportswear does male fashion change
    significantly.

293 ✤ Never wear anything you wore 20 lbs or ten
    years ago.

294 ✦ It's bad enough to see a man wearing a suit and no socks and much worse if he's not wearing a shirt.

295 ✦ Nothing averts attention more quickly than an older woman dressed as a figment of her own imagination.

296 ✦ A woman who wishes to be treated as an equal in her business must not manipulate using sexuality.

297 ✤ The climb up the social ladder in America should be undertaken without stepping on others as your rungs.

298 ✤ Do not attempt to impose morality of previous decades upon the present generation—try, instead, to interpret it.

299 ❖ "There is no such thing as too much couth."

—S.J. Perelman

300 ❖ Tell everything you know and you will not be invited back.

301 ❖ Do not pester.

302 ✢ In an argument that cannot be won, defer by
saying, "You know, you could be right."

303 ✢ The proper thing to say to a woman dressed
exactly like you at a social function is, "I admire
your taste."

304 ✤ A lady may ask one man to inform another of his open fly.

305 ✤ If giving your phone number is the only way to escape, give it one digit off.

306 ✤ Ask your escort's permission before dancing with another.

307 ✤ Never be a pall-bearer for someone you wouldn't have carried while alive.

308 ✤ At a funeral or a wedding, never cry more than the immediate relatives.

309 ✦ After a romantic break up, women tend to call and hang up, men tend to drive by. Do neither.

310 ✦ Never abandon a friend, especially for another friend.

311 ✦ If you break an engagement with a friend because you received a better offer, you should expect similar treatment.

312 ✤ It is almost impossible to change the table manners of an adult human being.

313 ✤ You may not criticize a woman's style of dress unless you are prepared to pay for a new wardrobe.

314 ✤ A woman who has been struck by a man should call the police immediately. And vice versa.

315 ✤ Violence is not accepted at any social level.

316 ✤ The only traditions worthy of perpetuating are those of kindness.

317 ✤ Take into consideration that the absolutes of
power and money do not so much corrupt as
they unmask.

318 ✤ Sharing knowledge is the highest form of
philanthropy.

319 ✤ It is an insult to humanity not to recycle.

320 ✤ If you haven't time to recycle, find the time to call a recycling service for pickup.

321 ✤ Never throw away anything useful. The Salvation Army is only a phone call away.

322 ✦ Grace is courage under pressure.

323 ✦ Judging others by color or any other grouping only devalues oneself.

324 ✦ If you have Spanish speaking help in your home, you should pay them extra to teach you their language.

325 ✤ Don't throw paint on fur coats if you are wearing leather shoes.

326 ✤ Anyone who can afford a Rolls-Royce should be driving an electric car.

327 ✤ Never volunteer for a project just for publicity.

328 ✤ The most successful people learn from their mistakes rather than repeat them.

329 ✤ If at all possible, avoid marrying anyone younger than your oldest child.

330 ✤ A woman discarded by her husband should not use revenge as the barometer for her next choice.

331 ✤ In a natural disaster such as earthquake, fire
or flood, all social barriers fall. Try to work this
adaptability into daily life.

332 ✤ Snobbery is artificial.

333 ✤ Social climbers often betray themselves with their
eagerness.

334 ✤ Never exaggerate your lineage.

335 ✤ Family lineage is not terribly important unless
you are marrying into royalty.

336 ✤ Your ancestors are not nearly as important as you.

337 ✤ Be proud of your origins, no matter how humble.

338 ✢ "No one can make you feel inferior without
   your consent."   —Eleanor Roosevelt

339 ✢ We are a global community; there is no place for
   prejudice.

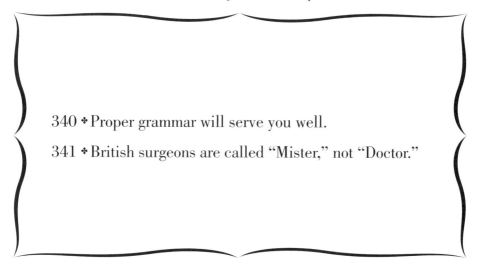

340 ❖ Proper grammar will serve you well.

341 ❖ British surgeons are called "Mister," not "Doctor."

342 ✤ If you don't agree, try to understand. If you can't understand, admit it.

343 ✤ The ancient tradition of *noblesse oblige* requires people of immense wealth to help the unfortunate.

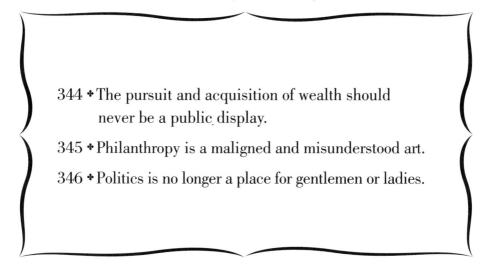

344 ✤ The pursuit and acquisition of wealth should never be a public display.

345 ✤ Philanthropy is a maligned and misunderstood art.

346 ✤ Politics is no longer a place for gentlemen or ladies.

347 ✤ Do not refer to a "weaker sex," as there no longer
is one.

348 ✤ Men and women alike can politely be assertive,
supportive or protective.

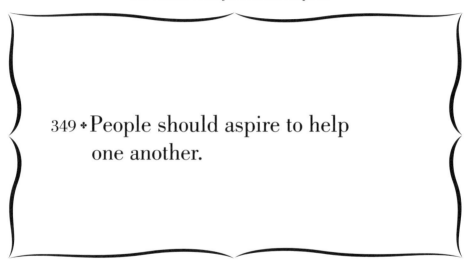

349 ✤ People should aspire to help one another.

350 ✦ Give credit where it is due.

351 ✦ Anything a woman does should be judged by the same standards by which a man would be judged.

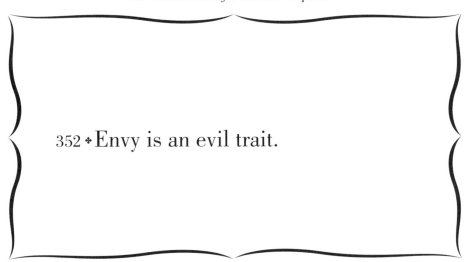

352 ✤ Envy is an evil trait.

353 ✦ Finger bowls are pretty useless. Just remember not to drink from them.

354 ✦ Um, hmmm, as a conversation device comes in very handy.

355 ❖ To those whose professed knowledge you know
to be false, the most you may do is invite them to
dinner with an expert in the field.

356 ❖ The art of revealing a poseur demands that only
the impostor knows he has been exposed.

357 ❖ The unkindest cut of all is to make sport of a
person who doesn't know the nature of the sport.

358 ❖ "Wit is perhaps the only weapon with which it is
possible to stab oneself in one's own back."
—Dorothy Parker

359 ✦ Blatant self-promotion usually backfires.

360 ✤ Politicians are no longer a rung in the social ladder.

361 ✤ In social life, consider good marriages to be more important than money or position.

362 ✤ Enormous wealth, no matter the nature of acquisition, holds immense responsibility.

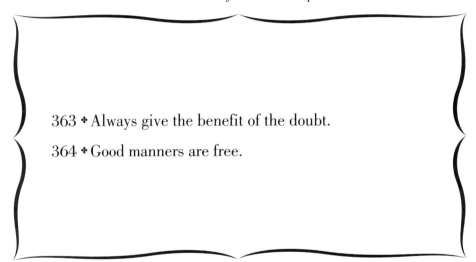

363 ✤ Always give the benefit of the doubt.

364 ✤ Good manners are free.

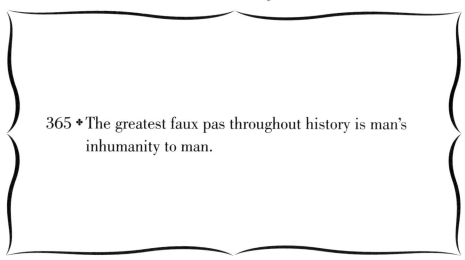

365 ✤ The greatest faux pas throughout history is man's inhumanity to man.

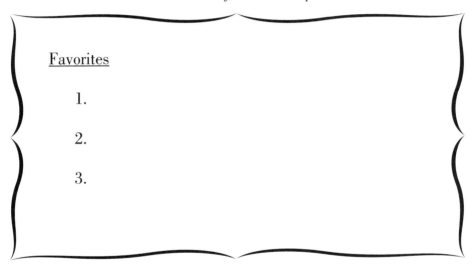

Favorites

    1.

    2.

    3.

4.

5.

6.